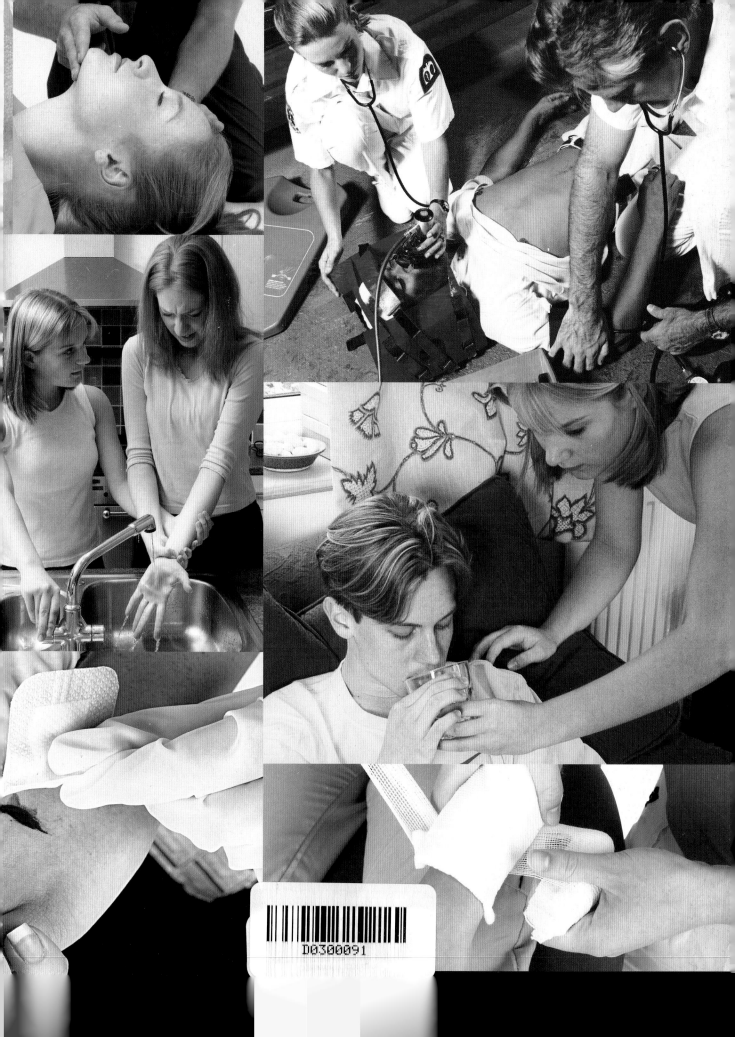

CONTENTS

INTRODUCTION

Learning basic first aid will prepare you for emergency situations and enable you to cope in a crisis. It is an important life skill that everyone should have, and this book will show you what to do in common first-aid situations. Some sections start with a simple rule. Learn the rules, and the treatment should make sense and be easy to remember.

Whenever you see this symbol in the book, it means there is nothing more you can do as a first-aider, and you are advised to contact the emergency services for further assistance.

Call an ambulance by dialling 999 (see page 5)

IN AN EMERGENCY

Getting help is not always the first thing to do in an emergency. If you can, assess the situation and the casualty, administer first aid and then get help. If you are not alone, get another person to ring the emergency services.

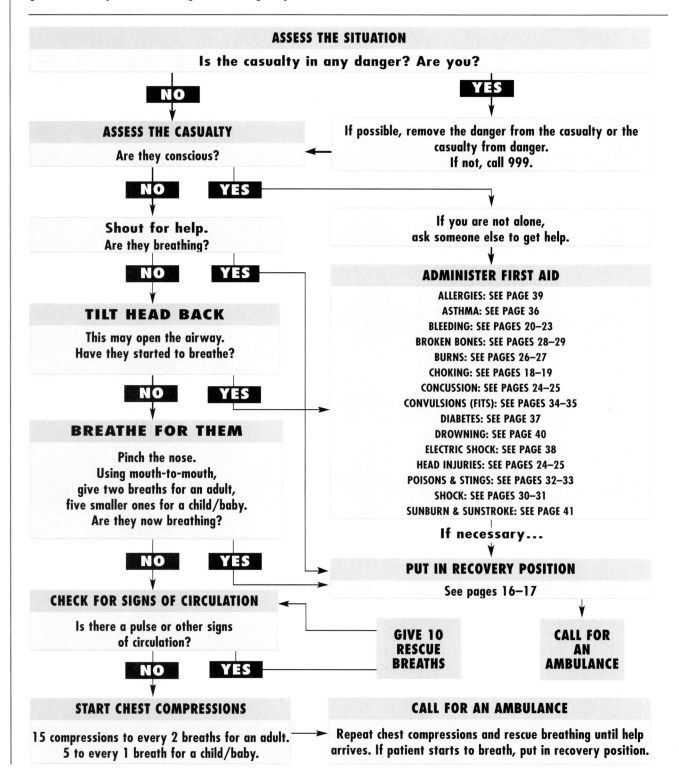

ASSESS THE SITUATION

Is the casualty in any danger? Are you?

NO   **YES**

If possible, remove the danger from the casualty or the casualty from danger.
If not, call 999.

ASSESS THE CASUALTY

Are they conscious?

NO   **YES**

If you are not alone,
ask someone else to get help.

**Shout for help.
Are they breathing?**

NO   **YES**

ADMINISTER FIRST AID

ALLERGIES: SEE PAGE 39
ASTHMA: SEE PAGE 36
BLEEDING: SEE PAGES 20–23
BROKEN BONES: SEE PAGES 28–29
BURNS: SEE PAGES 26–27
CHOKING: SEE PAGES 18–19
CONCUSSION: SEE PAGES 24–25
CONVULSIONS (FITS): SEE PAGES 34–35
DIABETES: SEE PAGE 37
DROWNING: SEE PAGE 40
ELECTRIC SHOCK: SEE PAGE 38
HEAD INJURIES: SEE PAGES 24–25
POISONS & STINGS: SEE PAGES 32–33
SHOCK: SEE PAGES 30–31
SUNBURN & SUNSTROKE: SEE PAGE 41

TILT HEAD BACK

**This may open the airway.
Have they started to breathe?**

NO   **YES**

BREATHE FOR THEM

Pinch the nose.
Using mouth-to-mouth,
give two breaths for an adult,
five smaller ones for a child/baby.
Are they now breathing?

If necessary...

PUT IN RECOVERY POSITION

See pages 16–17

NO   **YES**

CHECK FOR SIGNS OF CIRCULATION

Is there a pulse or other signs
of circulation?

**GIVE 10
RESCUE
BREATHS**

**CALL FOR
AN
AMBULANCE**

NO   **YES**

START CHEST COMPRESSIONS

15 compressions to every 2 breaths for an adult.
5 to every 1 breath for a child/baby.

CALL FOR AN AMBULANCE

Repeat chest compressions and rescue breathing until help
arrives. If patient starts to breath, put in recovery position.

CALLING THE EMERGENCY SERVICES

STEP 1
Pick up the phone and dial 999. You can also use 112. Try not to panic and speak clearly.

STEP 2
You will be asked WHICH EMERGENCY SERVICE YOU REQUIRE.

AMBULANCE • POLICE • FIRE • COASTGUARD
MOUNTAIN RESCUE • CAVE RESCUE

STEP 3
When connected, tell the emergency service...

- **WHAT THE EMERGENCY IS**
- **WHERE IT IS**
- **WHERE YOU ARE AND THE NUMBER OF THE PHONE YOU ARE USING**

CALLING THE DOCTOR

If the situation is not an emergency, you should call a doctor. If you can find out the number, call the patient's doctor. If not, call your own. If you cannot find either number, then call National Health Service Direct on:

0845 4647

STEP 4
Go back to help or observe, if you can, but MINIMISE THE DANGER TO YOURSELF. Your observations could help the emergency services when they arrive.

TOP TIP
Never make a false call. You risk the lives of others and it is illegal (you can be traced).

WHAT IS FIRST AID?

First aid is the immediate provision of treatment and care to a person who has suffered an illness or injury. It is often used before the emergency services or medical professionals take over. First aid is not an exact science but provided you stay within the rules, you can and will help the patient. The main thing to remember is that doing nothing is the worst thing you can do. Even calling for help or just comforting the patient can make a big difference to their chances of recovery.

THE BASIC RULES OF FIRST AID

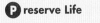

P reserve Life

P revent Worsening

P romote Recovery

All first-aiders use this rule to ensure that they do not miss anything out and that they treat the patient's conditions in the right order.

PRESERVE LIFE

Life-threatening situations are when the casualty is not breathing, when the heart has stopped beating or when there is severe bleeding. These conditions are the first-aiders top priority when treating the patient. This is when you must act, as you only have three minutes to get air into the lungs and blood circulating to the brain before permanent damage occurs. This book shows you what to do in these circumstances.

PREVENT WORSENING

Once you have ensured that the situation is not life-threatening or you have treated the patient successfully, then your next step is to prevent any worsening of the patient's condition. Stop the movement of broken bones, treat minor bleeding and burns, or treat the patient for shock.

PROMOTE RECOVERY

The final step in first aid is to assist the patient by getting any further help needed to give the patient the best chance of a full recovery. In many cases this will be getting the patient to medical professionals.

TOP TIP
Don't do nothing! You can and will make a difference if you follow these first aid rules.

ASSESSING THE SITUATION

D anger
R esponse
A irway
B reathing
C irculation

Making certain checks and acting on your findings will ensure that you have a good chance of preserving the patient's life. The basic rule is DR ABC (Doctor ABC).

PRESERVE LIFE

D anger
R esponse
A irway
B reathing
C irculation

Look, listen and smell. Danger comes in many forms so use all your senses to ensure that you and the casualty are not in any danger before you begin treatment.

eyes (look)   ears (listen)   nose (smell)

ASK FOR HELP

You are not expected to do everything. Bystanders can be used to help with tasks such as stopping traffic, calling an ambulance or going to get a first-aid kit.

MAKE THE AREA SAFE

Make the area safe. If the patient is in the road, get someone to park his or her car between the patient and oncoming traffic. Make sure they put on the handbrake and hazard lights.

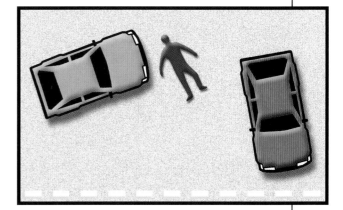

USE BYSTANDERS

Use bystanders to slow the traffic down or keep crowds back. Make sure they do not risk their own safety while assisting you.

ASSESS THE RISKS BEFORE YOU HELP

If the patient is in water, throw a rope or use a pole for them to hold on to. If you have to go into the water, make sure someone is on hand to help you or that you have something to hold on to that will help you get out again. People who are in trouble in water often panic, and this could jeopardise your safety too.

TOP TIP
Your safety is vital and at no time should you put yourself in danger.

ASSESSING THE CASUALTY

Now that the area is safe, the next thing to do is to assess the casualty. The things to look out for are signs of consciousness, breathing and circulation. Keep a mental note of the patient's responses, so you can pass on the information to the medical professionals when they arrive.

CHECKING RESPONSE

Assessing consciousness is done by checking the response of the casualty to sound and touch.

STEP 1 DANGER – Assess the situation. Is there any danger to you, the patient or to anyone else? Only proceed if it is safe to do so.

Danger
Response
Airway
Breathing
Circulation

Danger
Response
Airway
Breathing
Circulation

STEP 2 RESPONSE – Check to see if the patient is conscious. Kneel down next to them and tap their shoulders. Look at their face and talk loudly into both ears. Watch for any reactions or movements, particularly in the eyes, eyelids or mouth. If the person is conscious, ask what happened and assess any injuries. **If there is no reaction, go to STEP 3.**

Danger
Response
Airway
Breathing
Circulation

Often when a person loses consciousness, their head falls forward and the tongue slides to the back of the mouth. This blocks the airway and stops the patient breathing.

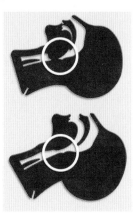

STEP 3 AIRWAY – Clear the patient's airway by lifting the jaw with two fingers while your other hand holds the top of the head. Listen and look for any sign of breathing for up to 10 seconds. If the patient begins to breathe, go to Step 6. **If not, shout for someone to call an ambulance and go to STEP 4.**

RESCUE BREATHING (MOUTH-TO-MOUTH)

- **D** anger
- **R** esponse
- **A** irway
- **B** reathing
- **C** irculation

STEP 4 BREATHING (ADULT) – *Check to see if the patient is breathing. Put your ear near their mouth and look down at the chest. If there is no reaction, pinch the patient's nose closed with your fingers. Seal your mouth over their opened mouth and blow firmly. As you breathe, look along the chest to check that it rises. Give another rescue breath. You may have to make up to five attempts to get two breaths into the patient as there may be a blockage in the airway.* **If they start to breathe, go to Step 6. If not, go to Step 5.**

STEP 5 CIRCULATION – *If you are alone and there is still no sign of breathing, call an ambulance. Repeat procedure immediately and then check for signs of circulation.* **See next page.**

STEP 6 *Put the patient in the recovery position (see pages 16–17) and call an ambulance. Wait with the patient until it arrives.*

BREATHING (CHILD) – *The procedure is the same for children and babies, but as their faces are smaller, you may have to cover both the mouth and nose with your mouth to get a seal. Remember to adjust the strength of your breath to only blow enough air into the patient to move their chest.* **If they start to breathe, go to Step 6. If not, go to Step 5.**

TOP TIP
Do not put your fingers into the patient's mouth to clear a blockage unless you can see it – you may force the blockage further down the airway.

CHECKING CIRCULATION

Your heart and blood vessels take oxygen to all parts of the body. If the heart stops then the first-aider must try to get the blood circulating within three minutes or permanent damage will start to occur.

WHAT TO LOOK FOR

At this stage, time is of the essence. First-aiders now look for signs of circulation rather than checking the pulse.

D anger
R esponse
A irway
B reathing
C irculation

STEP 1

The skin around the lips and eyes is the best place to look first. If the heart has stopped the skin will look ashen, be bluish in colour and feel damp. This is because the blood in the body contains no oxygen.

STEP 2

*Look closely for signs of circulation in the patient, such as normal breathing, coughing or movement. **If there are signs of circulation, commence rescue breathing (see page 11).***

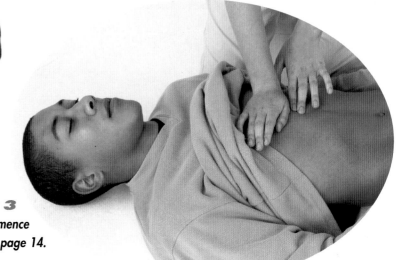

STEP 3

If there are no signs of circulation, commence chest compressions (CPR). Go to page 14.

TOP TIP
Checking for circulation is vital. If the heart has stopped, rescue breaths will have no effect.

THE PULSE

If there are signs of circulation then you can assess what the heart is doing by the regularity of the pulse and the strength of its beat.

CHECKING AN ADULT'S PULSE

The best place to find an adult's pulse is next to the windpipe on the neck. Use two fingers and press them along the side of the neck until you feel the pulse.

A pulse can also be found on the wrist (see page 31) but this is not as easy to find.

CHECKING A CHILD'S PULSE

Check the child's pulse as you would an adult's, but you may only have to use one finger.

MONITORING THE PULSE

Check the casualty's pulse every minute for 10 seconds. Record the number of beats and the strength of the pulse. The pulse should average 60–80 beats per minute, which is 10–13 beats per 10 seconds. If possible, write down your observations and inform the emergency services or hospital.

CHECKING A BABY'S PULSE

Babies have not developed the cartilage that protects the airway in the neck. It is therefore safer to check the pulse by using two fingers on the inside of the upper arm.

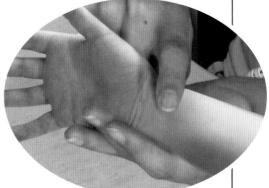

CHEST COMPRESSIONS (CPR)

If there is no circulation, you must get the blood circulating by pressing the heart. The chest and ribs are flexible and this allows you to press the chest down until the heart is squeezed. This means that the chest will be compressed to by four to five centimetres. Once you have learnt the techniques, practise on a pillow using a watch to get yourself used to the speed.

Danger
Response
Airway
Breathing
Circulation

CHEST COMPRESSIONS ON AN ADULT

STEP 1 Ensure that the patient is lying flat on their back on a hard surface.

STEP 2 Expose the chest and run your fingers along the ribs until you find the point where they join the breastbone. Measure two finger-widths above this point and place the heel of your hand on the breastbone.

CPR RATIOS
ADULT 15:2
Fifteen compressions to two breaths. Use two hands.

CHILD 5:1
Five compressions to every one breath. Use one hand.

BABY 5:1
Five compressions to every one breath. Use two fingers.

STEP 3 Put your other hand on top. Press down firmly and quickly 15 times. You should do the 15 compressions in just under 10 seconds.

STEP 4 Give two rescue breaths (see page 11). Start this sequence as soon as you can and keep doing the compressions and rescue breathing until the patient begins to breathe on their own or until the ambulance arrives.

CHEST COMPRESSIONS ON A CHILD

If the patient is between one and eight years old, place the heel of one hand just slightly above where the ribs join the breastbone. Press down firmly and quickly five times, followed by one rescue breath. Continue until the child begins to breathe. If the child is aged nine or older, treat as for an adult.

CHEST COMPRESSIONS ON A BABY

For a baby, you will need only two fingers. Place them just slightly above where the ribs join the breastbone and press down firmly and quickly, followed by one rescue breath. You can do these compressions by holding the baby on your arm. This is useful as you can phone for an ambulance at the same time. Remember to keep the airway open by tilting the head back. Continue until the baby begins to breathe.

TOP TIP
Keep the patient's clothes on if it would cause delay to remove them.

THE RECOVERY POSITION

I f the unconscious patient is breathing and has signs of circulation, it is important to maintain the
open airway. Putting them into the recovery position will do this safely. The only time you should
leave an unconscious casualty on their back is if you suspect they have suffered a broken back or
neck. In this case, just keep the airway open by tilting the head up.

INTO THE RECOVERY POSITION

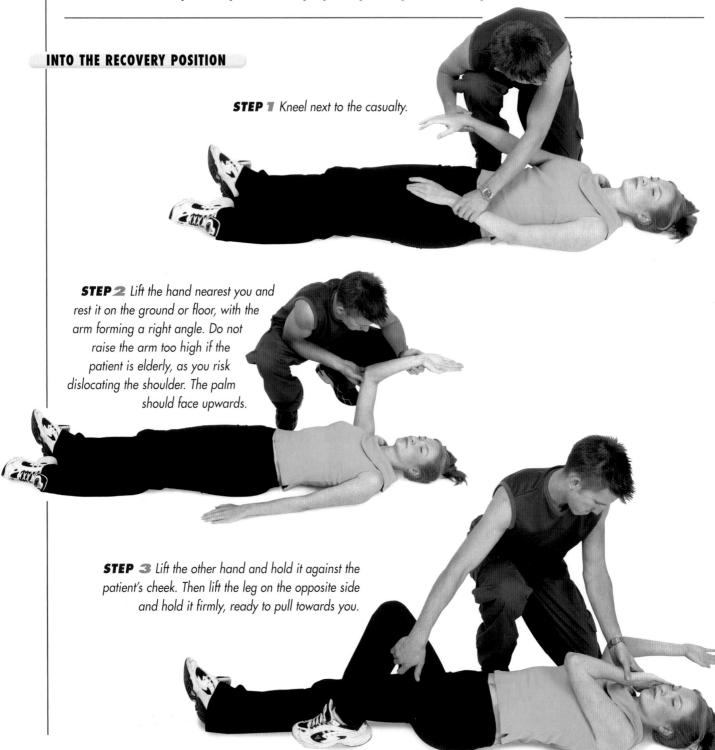

STEP 1 Kneel next to the casualty.

STEP 2 Lift the hand nearest you and
rest it on the ground or floor, with the
arm forming a right angle. Do not
raise the arm too high if the
patient is elderly, as you risk
dislocating the shoulder. The palm
should face upwards.

STEP 3 Lift the other hand and hold it against the
patient's cheek. Then lift the leg on the opposite side
and hold it firmly, ready to pull towards you.

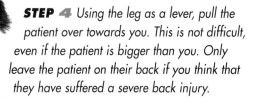

STEP 4 *Using the leg as a lever, pull the patient over towards you. This is not difficult, even if the patient is bigger than you. Only leave the patient on their back if you think that they have suffered a severe back injury.*

STEP 5 *Now that the patient is on their side, pull the top leg up until it is at a right angle to the body.*

STEP 6 *Open up the airway by lifting the chin and tilting back the head.*

TOP TIP
Use this position for unconscious casualties once you are sure that they are breathing.

CHOKING

Choking occurs when an object gets stuck in the back of the mouth or in the airway. This causes the body to react to the lack of oxygen in the lungs. The body normally clears the blockage by coughing. If this does not work then the first-aider must help quickly.

BLOCKED WINDPIPE

A blocked windpipe is a common occurrence which can cause major problems unless treated quickly. The blockage is usually food or something that a person has put into their mouth.

IF AN ADULT IS CHOKING

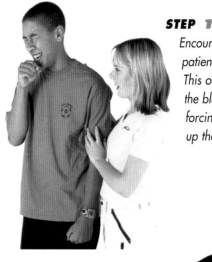

STEP 1

Encourage the patient to cough. This often loosens the blockage by forcing air back up the windpipe.

STEP 2

If this does not work then slap the patient firmly between the shoulder blades. Put your other hand on their chest as this will help support them and compress the chest. Do this up to five times.

STEP 3

If the blockage has not cleared, you need to do abdominal thrusts. Stand behind the patient and link your arms around the abdomen. Pull sharply towards you and upwards. Try this five times, along with backslaps, until the airway clears.

STEP 4

If the patient loses consciousness, slowly lower them to the ground and start rescue breathing and CPR (see pages 11 and 14). This should clear any obstruction that is lodged in the throat.

IF A CHILD IS CHOKING

Choking is very common in children as they often put small objects in their mouths, which can easily get stuck in their airway.

STEP 1 If a child starts to choke, slap them firmly on the back between the shoulder blades. Put your other hand on their chest as this will help support them and compress the chest. Do this up to five times.

STEP 2 If this does not work, you need to attempt abdominal thrusts on the child. **See page 18, step 3.**

STEP 3 If this does not work and the child loses consciousness, lower them gently to the ground.

STEP 4 Compress the chest quickly and sharply with one hand, which should force air out of the lungs up the airway. (This method can also be tried before the child loses consciousness). Get someone to call an ambulance. Start rescue breathing and CPR (see pages 11 and 15).

IF A BABY IS CHOKING

If a baby starts to choke, lay them face down along the length of the arm. Use your other hand to administer slaps between the shoulder blades. If the baby starts to lose consciousness then commence rescue breathing and CPR (see pages 11 and 15).

TOP TIP
You must not do abdominal thrusts on a baby under one year old.

BLEEDING

Bleeding often looks worse than it really is. The first-aider's task is to start treatment quickly before the loss of blood causes the patient to suffer from clinical shock (see pages 30–31). Treat bleeding by applying direct pressure over the wound, bandaging firmly and raising the part of the body that is bleeding.

GENERAL TREATMENT

STEP 1 Calm the patient down and encourage them to sit or lie down. Ask the patient to apply pressure to the wound with their hand, and elevate the wound. Wear sterile gloves if possible to minimise any risk of infection.

STEP 2 Assess the wound. If it is a small cut, go to Step 3. If it is a large wound, go to Step 4. If there is a foreign body in the wound, or if you suspect the bone is broken, go to Step 6.

STEP 3 Wash your hands and then clean the wound with clean running water or an alcohol-free wipe. Get an adhesive dressing (plaster) from your first-aid box. The dressing should be big enough for the sterile pad to completely cover the wound.

STEP 4 If it is a large wound, you will need to use a field dressing. Open the sealed package and unroll the short side of the bandage. Hold the dressing onto the wound and wrap the long side of the bandage around the limb. Tie the long and short ends together. If you do not have a field dressing or bandage, you could use a clean, non-fluffy piece of material.

STEP 5 If the bleeding does not stop, tie a second bandage over the first. Get the patient to hospital or call an ambulance. If the wound is still bleeding, remove both bandages and start again with a fresh bandage.

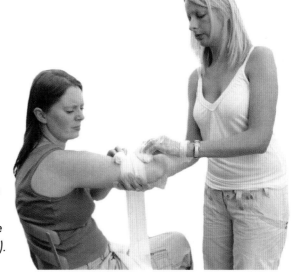

STEP 6 If there is a bone or foreign object in the wound, cover it lightly. Pad either side and then apply the bandage. The pads will ensure the bandage doesn't press on the object. Even if you are not certain that the bone is broken, do not move the limb. Dress the wound on the arm without moving the arm and make a sling (see pages 28–29).

LEG WOUND

For a leg wound, apply a sterile dressing then raise the injured leg to get blood flowing back towards the heart.

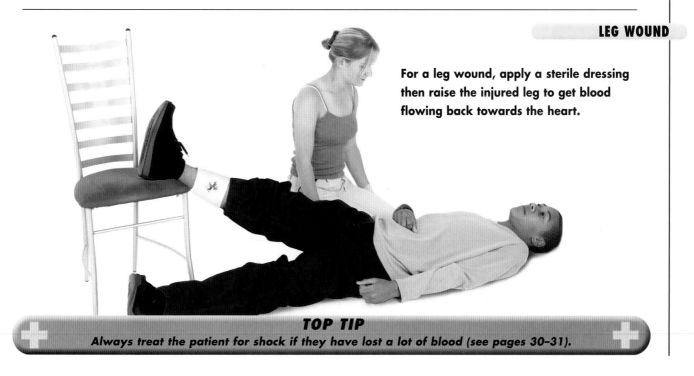

TOP TIP
Always treat the patient for shock if they have lost a lot of blood (see pages 30–31).

BLEEDING FROM THE HEAD

Cuts on the head bleed a lot but the treatment is the same as for any wound. If there is blood or any other fluid coming from inside the ear, this may mean that there is internal bleeding. This must be treated carefully, as stopping the bleeding may cause pressure to build up within the brain cavity (see page 25).

HEAD CUT

Any cut on the head must be treated by applying a clean dressing. Reposition any loose flaps of skin then secure with the dressing.

STEP 1 *Use a triangular bandage by placing the long edge on the head above the eyebrows. The point should fall down the back of the neck. Draw both ends to the middle and cross them over.*

STEP 2 *Bring the two ends round the front and tie a knot on the forehead. Pull the point at the back down to gently tighten the bandage, then secure on the head with a safety pin or tuck it into the folds.*

BLEEDING FROM THE MOUTH

Bleeding from the inside of the mouth can be stopped by getting the patient to hold a small sterile pad against the wound. This works for cuts on the cheek, tongue or from a tooth cavity. If the bleeding continues for more than 10 minutes, get the patient to a hospital.

BLEEDING FROM THE NOSE

Bleeding from the nose is treated by getting the patient to sit down, lean forward and pinch the nose just below the end of the bone. Remind the patient to breathe through their mouth. The bleeding should have stopped after 10 minutes, but if it hasn't, continue to pinch the nose. If the bleeding continues for more than 30 minutes, you should get the patient to a hospital.

If you are unsure whether a wound is external or internal, treat as an internal head injury (see page 25). If it is the ear lobe that is bleeding, you will need to apply a field dressing.

Use the field dressing to cover the wound and bind it around the head. Make sure that you do not cover the patient's eyes.

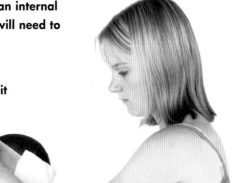

BLEEDING FROM THE EYE

This is often painful and very frightening. It could be a cut, a burst blood vessel or something more severe. Treat for a head injury (see page 25) if in any doubt. Either way, the wound needs to be dressed to prevent infection. Remember the patient may not be able to see clearly so tell them what you are going to do.

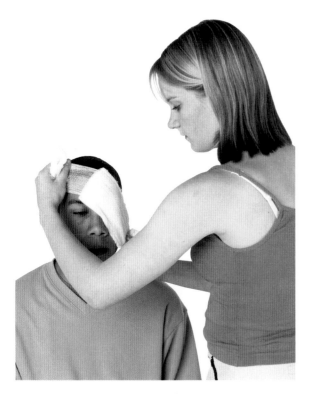

STEP 1 *Place a dressing lightly over the eye, at an angle, with the pad completely covering the eye.*

STEP 2 *Wrap the dressing around the head, being careful not to cover the other eye. Ensure that you do not move too much in front of the patient as this can make the eyes move and cause further discomfort. Either get the patient to hospital or call an ambulance.*

TOP TIP
If your patient feels dizzy or loses consciousness, call an ambulance quickly.

CONCUSSION & SERIOUS HEAD INJURIES

All head injuries must be treated as serious and the patient should receive professional attention. While administering first aid, check on the patient's awareness to sound and touch.

CONCUSSION

The brain is surrounded by the skull for protection. When the head is hit with a hard object or bumped against a hard surface, the brain is shaken within the skull. This can cause a temporary condition called concussion. The patient may be confused, dizzy or may even lose consciousness.

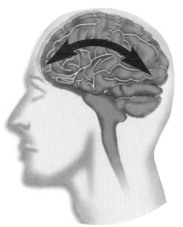

STEP 1 *Treat concussion by getting the patient to rest with the head raised. They may be able to sit on the ground, but if they feel dizzy then you must get them to lie down and raise their head by putting a blanket or coat underneath it.*

STEP 2 *The patient's level of awareness should increase and they should begin to react to touch and sound. Keep monitoring them for a few hours. If their awareness does not improve, there could be internal bleeding. Call an ambulance or get the patient to hospital immediately.*

BLEEDING FROM THE EAR & EYE

Bleeding from inside the ear or eye should be handled with care. If the blood is mixed with clear fluid it means that there is damage to tissue inside the brain cavity.

Bleeding from the ear or eye may come from inside the skull. If this is the case you will not be able to see the wound. Any wounds inside the head are serious as loss of blood supply to the brain or pooling of blood within the skull will become life threatening. Keep the patient still and treat as for a head injury.

HEAD INJURY

A head injury needs to be treated very carefully. Always assume that a person with a head injury has injured their neck as well.

STEP 1 *If the patient is conscious, get them to lie flat on their back and keep them as still as you can. Ring for an ambulance immediately.*

STEP 2 *If you have to leave the patient to ring an ambulance, put them in the recovery position (see pages 16–17).*

(see pages 16–17).

TOP TIP
Keep monitoring the casualty's reaction to your voice. If their level of awareness or responses starts to decline then call an ambulance quickly.

BURNS

Burns can be caused by heat, friction, electric shock or chemicals. Burnt areas become red and swollen, often with blisters on the skin. Burns caused by heat can continue to burn even after the source of heat has been removed.

SCALDING

Scalding is caused by very hot substances or objects touching the skin. The most common place for scalding accidents is in the kitchen, with boiling water and hot pans being a particular risk.

STEP 1 Make sure the area is safe for you and your patient before you start the treatment. Turn the heat off and move the patient away from any danger.

STEP 2 Wash the burnt area with cold running water for at least 10 minutes. If the patient is still in pain, continue for a further 10 minutes.

STEP 3 Once the burnt area is thoroughly cool, cover with a triangular dressing or some non-fluffy material. A pillow case or even plastic clingfilm can be used.

STEP 4 If more than 5% of the patient's skin area has been burnt, they should attend Casualty. This could be the equivalent of the lower half of an arm.

Electrical burns are caused by electricity flowing through the patient. The burns may not be visible but the patient will be in pain. Only touch them once you are sure that they are not touching anything connected to the electricity. Remember that metal fixtures conduct electricity.

STEP 1 *Switch off and unplug the electrical appliance. Don't touch the patient until you are sure that the flow of electricity has been cut off. You may need to call the electricity company if the source is a pylon or substation.*

STEP 2 *Treat as you would for scalding. Go to Step 2 on page 26.*

CHEMICAL BURNS

Some dangerous chemicals burn the skin on contact. All dangerous chemicals should have a warning label on them. Make a note of the name and code on the label and tell the ambulance and hospital staff. This will help them to treat the patient correctly.

STEP 1 *Use gloves to move the chemicals out of the way.*

STEP 2 *Wash the wound with running water for at least 20 minutes. Make sure that the water and any chemicals run away from the patient's body and yourself. Put a sterile dressing over the area and get medical attention.*

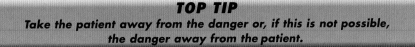

TOP TIP
Take the patient away from the danger or, if this is not possible, the danger away from the patient.

BROKEN BONES

The aim when treating a broken bone is to bind the limb in the position in which you find it. Do not try to straighten the bones as this will be done at the hospital. The first-aider's job is to prevent any further injury by limiting movement.

ASSESSING THE PATIENT

Unless a bone is protruding, it can be difficult to diagnose that it is broken. The patient will be in pain and unable to move the suspected break. If you are in any doubt, bind the limb to the body or support it in any way you can, and get the patient to hospital for an X-ray.

BROKEN ARM

For a suspected broken arm, you will need to make a sling using a triangular bandage. The type of sling will depend on the position the patient is holding the arm.

ELEVATED ARM SLING

If the arm is being held up to the shoulder, then make an elevated arm sling.

STEP 1 Check to see if there is any wound and pad around any bones that are sticking out (see page 21). Place the bandage over the arm with the point towards the elbow.

STEP 2 Tuck the bandage under the arm and twist it. Take it around the patient's back and up to the uninjured shoulder.

STEP 3 Tie the bandage at the shoulder. The patient should not be able to move the injured arm.

STEP 1 Tuck the bandage under the arm with the point to the elbow.

If the arm is being held towards the waist, use a lower arm sling.

STEP 2 Collect the point at the bottom and bring it over the shoulder of the injured arm. Bring the uppermost point around the back of the neck and tie a knot.

STEP 3 Fold the point around the elbow and pin the end to the bandage.

WRISTS, ANKLES, FINGERS, TOES & LEGS

Identifying broken bones is often difficult. If there is any doubt then treat the injury as a break.

WRIST OR FINGERS – pad any protruding bones and use a lower arm sling.

TOES – carefully place a loose shoe or sandal on the foot with the help of the patient and then take them to hospital.

ANKLES – take any weight off the ankle by helping the patient to walk or sit down. Encourage them to rest the ankle and arrange for them to get to hospital.

LEGS – first check for and treat any wound, trying to keep the leg in it's original position. Place padding between the knees and ankles and then call an ambulance. If the area is unsafe and you have to move the patient, bind the legs together first. Move the uninjured leg towards the broken one and tie bandages above and below the break and at the knees and ankles.

SHOCK

The medical condition known as shock is caused by the loss or pooling of body fluids away from the vital organs in the head and chest. Most injuries, including bleeding, broken bones and burns, result in the patient suffering from shock. If left untreated, it can be fatal as the body begins to 'shut down' its vital functions.

SIGNS OF SHOCK

The skin will be paler than normal and feel damp. Breathing may be shallow and fast and the patient's pulse will be rapid but weak.

TREATING SHOCK

The rule for treating shock is:

Warmth
Air
Rest
Talk

STEP 1

Get the patient to rest by helping them to lie down. Ensure that there is something warm such as a blanket or coat between the patient and the ground. This is more important than covering the patient as more heat is lost into the ground than up from the body.

STEP 2

Loosen tight clothing to help the patient breathe freely.

Warmth
Air
Rest
Talk

STEP 3

Raise the patient's legs in the air and support them with a blanket or a stool. This will allow the blood to flow back to the vital organs. If you think that they are losing consciousness or their injuries are severe, call an ambulance.

Warmth
Air
Rest
Talk

STEP 4

Do not give the patient anything to eat or drink.

STEP 5

Reassure the patient and continue to talk and listen to him or her until help arrives.

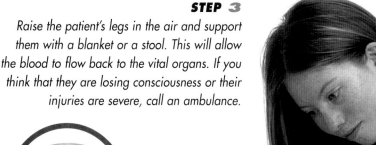

Warmth
Air
Rest
Talk

MONITORING THE PATIENT

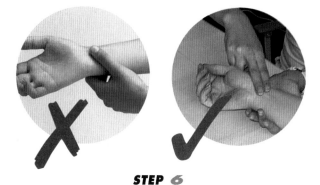

STEP 6

Check the pulse every minute, using your fingers over the wrist (see page 13). Do not use your thumb to feel the pulse as your thumb has a pulse of its own.

STEP 7

If you can, record the results and any useful observations to tell the emergency services.

POISONS & STINGS

Poisons are substances that are harmful to us. Even things that we use every day can be poisonous if taken in large quantities. Poisons can enter the body by the mouth, nose or through the skin.

TYPES OF POISON

Poisons can have many different effects on the body. Some may cause drowsiness while others may cause the patient to become very active and agitated. Others are corrosive and cause burns inside as well as outside the body. Many everyday products are poisonous if used in the wrong way.

SWALLOWED POISON

These are often pills or household fluids such as cleaning materials. Remember substances that are safe taken in small doses can be poisonous if swallowed in large quantities.

STEP 1 *Keep the patient calm. Wipe the mouth with a cloth to remove any traces of the poison. Find out whether the poison is corrosive (usually a liquid, such as bleach).*

STEP 2 *If the poison is corrosive, give the patient some cool water to sip to cool the throat.*

STEP 3 *Call for an ambulance and record pulse and breathing rates every five minutes. Keep any bottles to help the hospital to treat the patient. Never make the patient vomit.*

INHALED POISONS

Smoke or other gases cause a reduction of oxygen in the air and can poison the body. Your own safety is vital here and getting help quickly is often the first thing you should do.

STEP 1 *If the patient is conscious and coughing, call to them to come to you. If there is no response, then call the fire and ambulance emergency services. Assess the risks to your own safety before you attempt to help.*

STEP 2 If possible, help the patient to a safe area where there is fresh air. If they are unconscious, pull them to safety to commence ABC (see pages 10–15). If they are conscious then place them in the recovery position and monitor their pulse while waiting for the emergency services to arrive.

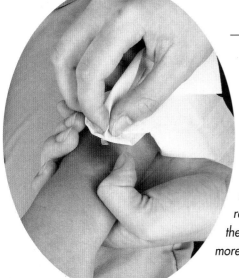

STINGS

Stings are another form of poison injected through the skin.

STEP 1 Sit the patient down and try to reassure them.

STEP 2 If you can see the sting, carefully remove it. Do not squeeze the area, as this will force more poison into the patient.

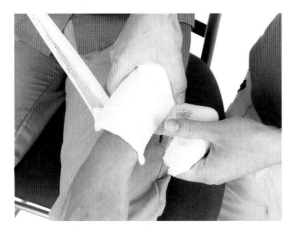

STEP 3 Wrap the area with a clean dressing and treat the patient for shock (see pages 30–31). If the patient starts to have difficulty breathing or the area starts to swell, get medical help or call an ambulance immediately.

TOP TIP
Do not put yourself in danger. You may have to get the emergency services to make the area safe before a fire victim can be rescued.

CONVULSIONS (FITS)

Many people suffer from convulsions, causing them to fall to the ground and jerk rapidly and violently. Convulsions are caused by erratic nervous impulses from the brain, triggered by strobe lighting, illness or other medical conditions. As a first-aider you cannot treat most of the causes, but quick action will stop the patient suffering injury during an attack.

CONVULSIONS IN ADULTS

Convulsions can be very frightening but do not panic. Make the area safe by moving anything out of the way that could harm the patient

STEP 1 Move whatever you can away from the patient but do not restrain them unless they are likely to hurt themselves.

STEP 2 If possible, put something soft under the patient's head.

STEP 3 Once the convulsion has run its course, place the patient into the recovery position (see pages 16–17). They may feel like sleeping, but when they wake up, let them rest and keep an eye on them.

CONVULSIONS IN BABIES

Many babies have convulsions because they are not yet able to control their body temperature. These attacks can occur between the ages of 6 months and 6 years old. When this happens the baby will feel very hot.

STEP 1
Stay calm and carefully remove the baby's clothing.

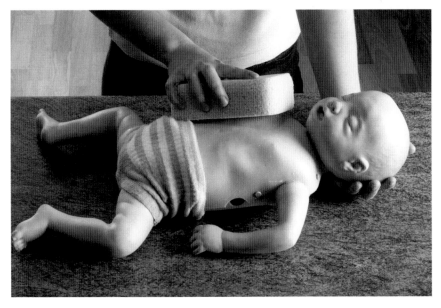

STEP 2 *Gently wipe the baby with a cool damp sponge and monitor their breathing. If the convulsion is prolonged commence ABC then call an ambulance. When the convulsions have stopped, reassure bystanders and parents, as this can be a distressing sight.*

MEDIC ALERT BRACELET

People with known conditions that can cause convulsions often wear medic bracelets or tags. If you find something like this, tell the emergency services.

TOP TIP
If the patient has more than one convulsion or if they have never had a convulsion before, call for an ambulance. If they have fully recovered, they should still see their doctor.

ASTHMA

Asthma is a common condition and sufferers usually have their own medication. If a sufferer should have an attack, all you may need to do is get their medication for them. It is important to act quickly to prevent their condition getting worse.

WHAT IS ASTHMA?

Asthma is a difficulty in breathing caused by the closing of the airways or a build-up of fluid in the lungs. Sufferers will have a shortness of breath and wheezing, appear pale and clammy and may show signs of exhaustion and anxiety. If treated quickly, the patient will easily recover.

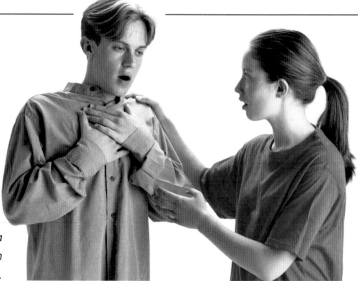

STEP 1 *Get the patient to sit down, preferably on a chair that is turned round. This will allow them to lean forwards to gather their breath.*

STEP 2 *Get the patient's medication for them. They should be able to use it themselves but if their attack is at an advanced stage, help them to take it by getting them to breathe in as you compress the inhaler. They should not need more than two puffs. Afterwards, ask the patient if they would like you to call an ambulance. In the event that you cannot obtain an inhaler, call an ambulance immediately. If their condition worsens, lay them on the floor and commence ABC (see pages 10–15).*

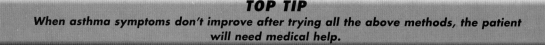

TOP TIP
When asthma symptoms don't improve after trying all the above methods, the patient will need medical help.

DIABETES

Diabetes is an imbalance of sugar in the body, caused by problems with the hormone insulin. A diabetic is unable to regulate their body sugar levels naturally and so often need to do so with medication. As a first-aider you are most likely to come into contact with a diabetic who has too little blood sugar.

DIABETIC WITH TOO LITTLE BLOOD SUGAR

A diabetic with too little blood sugar may start acting erratically or even have a fit. They may appear faint and weak and show signs of sweating followed by shallow breathing. If not treated quickly they may lose consciousness.

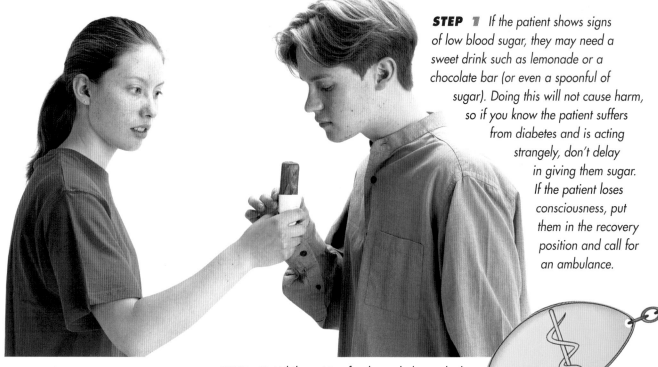

STEP 1 If the patient shows signs of low blood sugar, they may need a sweet drink such as lemonade or a chocolate bar (or even a spoonful of sugar). Doing this will not cause harm, so if you know the patient suffers from diabetes and is acting strangely, don't delay in giving them sugar. If the patient loses consciousness, put them in the recovery position and call for an ambulance.

STEP 2 While waiting for the ambulance, look for a medic alert bracelet to show the paramedics.

DIABETIC WITH TOO MUCH BLOOD SUGAR

A diabetic with too much blood sugar will have laboured breathing and a rapid pulse. They will start to lose consciousness over a period of several days and slip into a coma. Place them in the recovery position and call an ambulance for hospital treatment. Never attempt to give the casualty an insulin injection.

TOP TIP
You will not harm either type of diabetic by giving them sugar.

ELECTRIC SHOCK

Electric shock can have serious consequences for the casualty and put a first-aider and bystanders at great risk. It is important to act quickly in this situation.

TREATMENT

Electric shock can cause severe burns and heart failure, so isolate the casualty from the electrical source immediately.

STEP 1 *Turn off the main source of power if it is a household or general appliance. If this is not possible then remove the patient from the area using a non-conductive instrument such as a wooden broom or a rope.*

STEP 2 *Make sure that you do not move the patient to other electrical areas or places with water. Do not touch their skin before you have removed the electricity as the high voltage could give you a shock as well.*

STEP 3 *If the patient is burnt then treat for burns (see pages 26–27). If they are having breathing problems then place them on their back and commence ABC (see pages 10–15).*

999

TOP TIP
Alert people not to approach the scene of the accident.

ALLERGIES

There are many types of allergies but they are all caused by the body's sensitivity to substances that we normally consider to be harmless. These can be everyday allergies to dust, pollen, chemicals and food, or more serious reactions to drugs or venomous creatures.

GENERAL ATTACKS

The symptoms of an allergy are a rash, breathing difficulties or intestinal problems. It is difficult to identify the many allergies that people suffer from, but you can take steps to ease most symptoms.

STEP 1 *If a patient is vomiting then stay with them and give them fluids to rehydrate them. They may be hot and struggling for air.*

STEP 2 *If the patient is having difficulty breathing, allow them to sit in a comfortable position. If they begin to lose consciousness, help them to lie down. If the patient has an epipen (a self-medicating syringe containing adrenaline), help them to administer this.*

STEP 3 *Put them into the recovery position (see pages 16–17). Remember to ensure that the airway is open before calling for help.*

SERIOUS ATTACKS

999

STEP 4 *Call for an ambulance then continue to monitor the patient until it arrives. Be prepared to commence ABC (see pages 10–15).*

TOP TIP
Antihistamine cream or tablets will help rashes or minor breathing difficulties.

DROWNING

People can drown in a surprisingly small amount of water, even in a bath. If a person is in water and needs help, you must be careful that in their panic they do not pull you in.

GETTING THEM OUT OF THE WATER

If someone has fallen into the water or is in distress, keep calm but act quickly, shouting for help as you go. Never go into the water unless you are certain you will be safe.

STEP 1 See what is available around you to help with the rescue. Often there will be a life belt or rescue float with a rope tied to it. If this is the case, throw this to the person. Failing this, use a branch or pole instead.

STEP 2 Once the person gets hold of the object, pull them towards the edge and out of the water. Do not lean over to pull them out with your hands as they may pull you in.

STEP 3 If the person loses consciousness, check they are breathing. If not you will need to treat with rescue breaths (see page 11).

999

STEP 4 When they have started to breathe for themselves, put them in the recovery position and call for an ambulance.

TOP TIP
Only go into the water if you have help or can hold onto something. If you are a trained lifesaver, you must be sure there are no dangers in the water.

SUNBURN & SUNSTROKE

Sunburn is very common and painful. It is caused by over-exposure to the sun. In severe cases, it can lead to sunstroke where the body's temperature can become dangerously high.

Sunburn is characterised by red-hot skin, which sometimes blisters. Often the sufferer will be dehydrated.

STEP 1 Check the skin for any blisters.

STEP 2 If there are no blisters, gently wipe the area with a cool cloth or sponge. If there are blisters then treat the casualty for burns (see pages 26–27).

STEP 3 Get the patient into the shade and give them some water to sip slowly. This rehydrates them and will cool their body temperature. Never give them alcohol, tea or coffee to drink as these cause further loss of water.

- Keep well covered and wear a hat, even if there are clouds in the sky.
- Never fall asleep in the sun.
- If you are going to spend time in the sun, use a high-factor sun-protection cream.
- Drink plenty of water.

Sunstroke is the severe result of sunburn or overexposure to heat from the sun. The casualty may be confused or dizzy. Treat for sunburn and then call an ambulance. If the casualty loses consciousness then place them in the recovery position (see pages 16–17) before calling for an ambulance.

SAFETY

Millions of people are injured or killed every year by accidents. The most common cause of these is human error. The majority of accidents occur in the home by falling objects, collisions, explosions or falls. Road accidents also account for a large proportion of deaths and injuries, where speeding or dangerous driving are responsible. It is the first-aider's responsibility to help prevent accidents by using common sense to make the environment safe and secure.

SAFETY OUTDOORS

The garden is a prime area for accidents. See if you can find 10 potential accidents in this garden scene. *(See right for answers).*

The home is a prime area for accidents. See if you can find 10 potential accidents in this living room scene. *(See below for answers).*

In the home:

1) Toys in the hallway.
2) Water kept on top of a television set.
3) A cigarette on the arm of a flammable sofa.
4) An iron left face down on the ironing board.
5) A socket overloaded with plugs.
6) A fire left exposed without a guard.
7) A boiling pan left unattended.
8) A tea towel hanging above an open flame.
9) A knife left hanging over a kitchen surface.
10) A broken fire alarm.

In the garden:

1) A mower going over a live cable.
2) A bottle of poison left within reach of children.
3) An exposed rake.
4) A pair of shears left within reach of children.
5) Lighter fuel next to the flame of a barbecue.
6) A chainsaw left unattended.
7) A ladder leaning against a hedge.
8) Dog excrement left on the floor.
9) A loose paving slab.
10) An unguarded paddling pool.

REFRESHER COURSE

Call an ambulance, don't call an ambulance? Give him a slap on the back or a glass of water? Good first aid is about making the right decision in a crisis. You can do this by knowing the facts, so complete this checklist to see how well prepared you are.

QUESTIONS

You never know when you will face an emergency situation. However, the best approach to dealing with accidents and emergencies is to be prepared. Use this checklist to ensure that you understand what action to take in an emergency.

1. What is the first thing you should do if you see someone drowning?

a) Jump in to rescue them

b) Throw a rope or pole in for them to hold onto

c) Run and call for an ambulance

2. Where is the best place to check for a pulse on a child?

a) The wrist

b) The underarm

c) The neck

3. If somebody suffers a convulsion, what is the first thing you should do?

a) Move them into the recovery position

b) Hold their arms to restrain them

c) Move anything away from the patient that may cause injury

4. What is the first thing you should do if an adult is choking on a foreign object?

a) Perform an abdominal thrust

b) Begin rescue breathing

c) Encourage the patient to cough

5. If your friend has swallowed something poisonous, your first action should be to:

a) Give them some water to sip

b) Wipe their mouth clear of any traces of poison

c) Call an ambulance and collect any bottles they might have drunk from

6. What is the first thing you should do if someone suffers an electric shock?

a) Check that the patient has a pulse

b) Remove the source of the shock

c) Turn off the main source of power

7. Which of these injuries should you treat for internal bleeding?

a) Bleeding from the ear

b) A nosebleed

c) Bleeding from the mouth

1.

a) Never jump in to rescue them. They may pull you under in their panic, risking two lives instead of one.

b) **In this case you may be able to rescue them without the help of the emergency services, or enable them to float while you go to get help.**

c) This should be your second action after trying to assist the victim.

2.

a) There is a strong pulse in the wrist, but in an emergency situation it can be difficult to find.

b) The underarm is the safest place to find the pulse on a baby.

c) **This is the best place to find a pulse in an emergency.**

3.

a) Wait until the convulsion has run its course, then put the patient into the recovery position.

b) Do not restrain the patient unless they are likely to hurt themselves.

c) **This is the first thing you should do to ensure the patient does not hurt themselves further.**

4.

a) You should only do this if the patient has not been able to cough or if slapping their back has not worked, and you should never use this technique on a young child or baby.

b) If the choking patient loses consciousness, their airway is blocked. You will need to start CPR and rescue breathing.

c) **This is the first thing the patient should do, as the coughing reflex should release the object.**

5.

a) You should do this after you have cleared the traces of poison, just in case they swallow some more with the water.

b) **This is the first thing you should do to ensure the patient has no further contact with the poison.**

c) When your patient is calm and has had some water to drink, then call an ambulance.

6.

a) You should never touch the patient until you have removed the source of the shock, as the high voltage could shock you as well.

b) If you cannot turn the power off, remove the source of the shock with something that does not conduct electricity, such as a wooden broom or a piece of rope.

c) **This is the first thing to do to make sure the voltage is cut off.**

7.

a) **If you are unsure whether the wound is internal or external, treat the patient for an internal head injury.**

b) Nosebleeds are often caused by an external injury, but if the bleeding continues for more than 30 minutes, seek medical help.

c) Bleeding from the mouth does not indicate internal bleeding and should be treated by applying a sterile dressing to the wound.

FIRST-AID BOX

First-aid boxes contain all the essentials to administer first aid. Most public places should have a first-aid box by law, and many people have them in their homes and cars. If an accident occurs you should be able to find a well-equipped first-aid box. If not, there are many things around the house around the house that you can use.

WHAT'S IN THE BOX?

All the bandages and dressings should be wrapped to keep them sterile and should have a use-by date. Once this date has expired, they should be replaced.

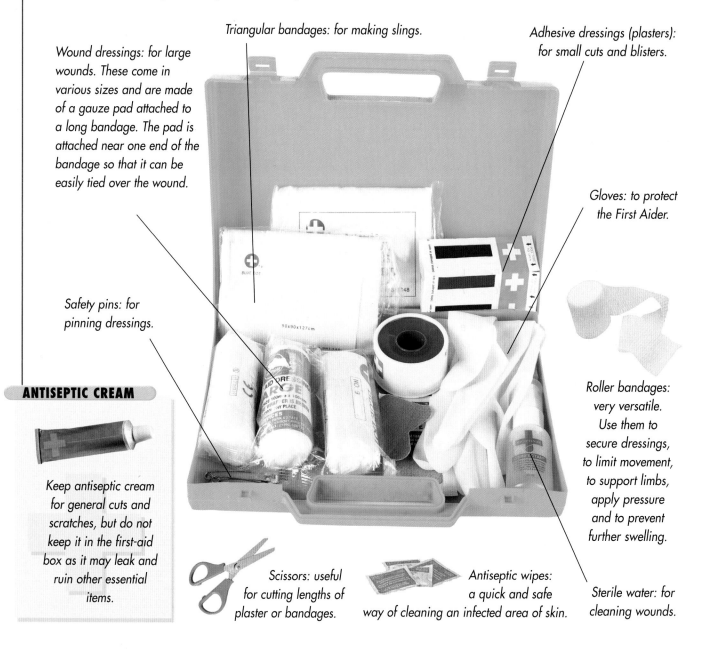

Triangular bandages: for making slings.

Wound dressings: for large wounds. These come in various sizes and are made of a gauze pad attached to a long bandage. The pad is attached near one end of the bandage so that it can be easily tied over the wound.

Adhesive dressings (plasters): for small cuts and blisters.

Gloves: to protect the First Aider.

Safety pins: for pinning dressings.

Roller bandages: very versatile. Use them to secure dressings, to limit movement, to support limbs, apply pressure and to prevent further swelling.

ANTISEPTIC CREAM

Keep antiseptic cream for general cuts and scratches, but do not keep it in the first-aid box as it may leak and ruin other essential items.

Scissors: useful for cutting lengths of plaster or bandages.

Antiseptic wipes: a quick and safe way of cleaning an infected area of skin.

Sterile water: for cleaning wounds.

HOUSEHOLD ALTERNATIVES

A sealed bottle of mineral water could be used to clean a wound.

If you do not have a first-aid box, you will need to be resourceful, looking around you to see what you could use instead. Many common objects can be put to good use in an emergency. However, it is important to make sure that substitute dressings are clean. Here are some suggestions:

A towel is a good source of padding for a broken leg that needs to be bound. Do not use on a wound or burn as the fibres will stick to it and contaminate it.

A necktie or scarf could make a sling or be used to elevate a bleeding arm or hand. Remember to tie it into a loop and ensure that it does not block the airway.

Use a tea towel to pad the dressing and prevent blood loss, or as a triangular dressing. Make sure that it is clean and not made of fluffy material.

Clingfilm can be used to cover a burn once the skin has cooled down.

A pillowcase could make a triangular bandage.

GLOSSARY

Airway – *The tube in the body that goes from the mouth and nose to the lungs.*

Abdominal Thrust – *The action used to help clear a blockage in the airway.*

Breathing – *The act of taking air into the lungs.*

Blisters – *Fluid collected under the skin usually caused by a burn.*

Circulation – *The flowing of blood from the heart through the arteries, veins and capillaries.*

Choking – *The body's natural reaction to a blockage in the airway.*

Convulsion – *Erratic movements cause by nervous activity within the brain. Also called a fit.*

Dehydration – *A lack of water in the body.*

Diabetes – *An imbalance of body sugars in the blood.*

Epilepsy – *A medical condition that results in the loss of awareness or convulsions.*

Fit – *See convulsion.*

Hazard Warning – *Signs that warn of danger. They include signs on poisons and corrosive substances.*

Infection – *Contamination of part of the body by a virus or bacteria.*

Lungs – *The organs in the chest where oxygen is directed to the blood and carbon dioxide is passed out.*

Medic Alert Bracelets – *Tags that are worn by people to indicate a specific medical condition.*

Oxygen – *Gas found in the air that the body needs to function.*

Rescue Breathing – *Breathing into the non-breathing patient to assist in recovery.*

Scald – *A burn caused by hot water or steam.*

Symptoms – *The signs of an illness or injury.*

Temperature (body) – *This is usually 36–38 degrees centigrade (97–100 degrees Fahrenheit)*

Unconsciousness – *A living state where the body shows no awareness of sight, sound or touch.*

Vomiting – *The expelling of substances from the digestive system.*

Windpipe – *The airway going from the nose and back of the mouth to the lungs.*

X-Ray – *A picture that shows the structure under the skin, usually taken to show the bones.*

ACKNOWLEDGEMENTS

ticktock Media Ltd.
Unit 2, Orchard Business Centre, North Farn Road, Tunbridge Wells, Kent TN2 3XF
Copyright © 2006 *ticktock* Media Ltd
First published in Great Britain by *ticktock* Media Ltd.
A CIP catalogue record for this book is available from the British Library. ISBN 1 86007 615 7
Photography by Roddy Paine Photographic Studios. Illustrations by John Aslton.

Picture Credits: Corbis: 7b

Printed in China. 2 3 4 5 6 7 8 9 10